OUR FAMILY RECIPES

PETER PAUPER PRESS, INC.
WHITE PLAINS, NEW YORK

PETER PAUPER PRESS
Fine Books and Gifts Since 1928

Our Company

In 1928, at the age of twenty-two, Peter Beilenson began printing books on a small press in the basement of his parents' home in Larchmont, New York. Peter—and later, his wife, Edna—sought to create fine books that sold at "prices even a pauper could afford."

Today, still family owned and operated, Peter Pauper Press continues to honor our founders' legacy—and our customers' expectations— of beauty, quality, and value.

Illustrations © Lindsay Dale

Additional art used under license from Shutterstock.com

Designed by David Cole Wheeler

Visit us at www.peterpauper.com

CONTENTS

INTRODUCTION

Family faces are magic mirrors. Looking at people who
belong to us, we see the past, present, and future.

Gail Lumet Buckley

There are some family recipes that are passed down over gen-
erations, and there are some that are born anew each year.
Whether it's Grandma's green bean casserole, or Aunt May's
perfect peach pie, certain dishes can magically transport us to a
different moment in time. A time where family gathered together
to share laughter, love, and a delicious meal! Keep hold of all
your treasured family recipes—past, present, and future—in this
recipe journal.

Record the recipe, the source, and why it holds special meaning
for your family. Convenient write-in Index pages for each category
enable you to locate recipes quickly. You'll also find tips, reference
charts, and kitchen hints to help you create that next heirloom recipe.

Bon appétit!

HELPFUL INFORMATION

Liquid Measures	Fluid Ounces	Metric
1 teaspoon	0.16	5 ml
1 tablespoon = 3 teaspoons	0.5	15 ml
1 ounce	1.0	30 ml
1/4 cup = 4 tablespoons	2.0	60 ml
1/3 cup = 5 tablespoons + 1 teaspoon	2.6	80 ml
1/2 cup = 8 tablespoons	4.0	120 ml
1 cup = 16 tablespoons	8.0	240 ml
2 cups = 1 pint	16.0	480 ml
4 cups = 1 quart	32.0	950 ml
4-1/4 cups	34.0	1 liter *(approx.)*
4 quarts = 16 cups = 1 gallon	128.0	3.78 liter

Dry Measures	Ounces by Weight	Metric
3 teaspoons = 1 tablespoon	0.5	14.3 grams
2 tablespoons = 1/8 cup	1.0	28.35 grams
4 tablespoons = 1/4 cup	2.0	56.7 grams
5-1/3 tablespoons = 1/3 cup	2.6	75.6 grams
8 tablespoons = 1/2 cup	4.0	113.4 grams
12 tablespoons = 3/4 cup	6.0	170 grams
16 tablespoons = 1 cup = ½ pound	8.0	227 grams
32 tablespoons = 2 cups = 1 pound	16.0	453.6 grams

Fahrenheit	Celsius	Gas Mark (U.K.)
250°	120°/130°	1/2
275°	140°	1
300°	150°	2
325°	160°/170°	3
350°	180°	4
375°	190°	5
400°	200°	6
425°	220°	7
450°	230°	8
475°	240°	9
500°	260°	10

(Approximate equivalents)

STORAGE & FREEZER TIPS

- Keep refrigerator temperature between **34° F** (1 C°) and **40° F** (4 C°).
- Keep freezer temperature at **0° F** (-17° C).
- Always thaw frozen foods in the refrigerator or microwave. Follow manufacturer's instructions for microwave thawing of foods. Thawing food at room temperature promotes bacterial growth.
- Never refreeze food that has been thawed.
- Keep uncooked meat, poultry, and fish in the coldest part of the refrigerator. Use within 1–2 days, or freeze.
- Do not wash fresh fruits and vegetables before storing them in the refrigerator. Store loosely to allow air to circulate. Wash thoroughly immediately before using.
- Many dry foods such as ground coffee, spices, and flour will stay fresher if refrigerated in an air-tight container.
- Except for ice cream, dairy products do not freeze well.
- Never freeze eggs in the shell—they will burst.

COOKING HINTS

- When measuring ingredients, level off dry measures with the flat blade of a knife. Measure liquids on a level surface.
- Flour increases in volume after sifting, so measure before sifting.
- A little lemon juice will prevent produce such as avocados and apples from turning brown.
- A meat thermometer will help ensure properly cooked meats.
- Do onions make you cry? Try refrigerating them until just before use.

USING THE MICROWAVE

- Never use metal containers or utensils in the microwave.
- Avoid cooking foods with high fat content in the microwave.
- When cooking in the microwave, turn or stir foods halfway through the cooking time to ensure even cooking throughout.

- Small, uniform-sized pieces of food will cook more quickly and evenly than large or irregularly-shaped pieces.
- Covering food while cooking or reheating helps retain moisture.

HEALTHIER COOKING

- Whenever you can, substitute olive oil for butter and other fats.
- Experiment with different types of lettuce. Leaf lettuce and spinach contain more nutrients than iceberg lettuce.
- Choose fresh vegetables over frozen, frozen over canned.
- Stir-frying, grilling, and steaming bring out the flavor in vegetables. Add zest with fresh herbs.
- Canned foods often contain added salt. If using in recipes, reduce salt accordingly.

COMPATIBLE HERBS & SPICES FOR SAVORY DISHES

- **Beef**: basil, bay, coriander/coriander seeds, cumin, dill, marjoram, sage, tarragon, thyme
- **Fish**: anise, basil, caraway, chives, dill, fennel, lemon balm, parsley, rosemary, sage, tarragon, thyme
- **Lamb**: bay, caraway, coriander/coriander seeds, cumin, dill, marjoram, mint, rosemary, sage, thyme
- **Pork**: anise, basil, chervil, coriander/coriander seeds, cumin, dill, fennel, lemon balm, marjoram, mint, rosemary, sage, tarragon, thyme
- **Poultry**: basil, bay, caraway, coriander/coriander seeds, cumin, dill, lemon balm, mint, parsley, rosemary, sage, tarragon, thyme

WINE PAIRINGS

- **Rule of thumb:** Serve light wines with light foods and heavy wines with heavy foods.
- **Meats, cheeses, other fatty, protein-rich foods:** Cabernet Sauvignon, red Bordeaux
- **Salty foods and less sweet desserts:** sweet Rieslings, white Zinfandel, dessert wines
- **Salty, oily, or fatty foods:** dry Rieslings, Chablis, Sauvignon Blanc

GLOSSARY OF COOKING TERMS

al dente: slightly undercooked (referring to pasta)

bain-marie: a large, shallow pan of warm water, holding a container of food, which is thus surrounded with gentle heat. This technique is designed to cook delicate dishes slowly and gently without breaking or curdling them. It can also be used to keep cooked foods warm.

baste: to moisten meat or fish with fat or liquid during cooking, to prevent drying out

blanch: to immerse vegetables or meat in boiling water for a few moments

braise: to cook food slowly in a covered pan over low heat with a small amount of liquid

brine: to immerse, preserve, or pickle in salt water (and sometimes additional sweeteners or herbs)

crudités: raw seasonal vegetables, frequently accompanied by a dipping sauce, often served as an appetizer

cube: to cut food into small, evenly sized cubes

cut in: to blend fat and flour together with a pastry blender, or two knives, until the mixture forms coarse crumbs of uniform size

dash: a very small amount, less than 1/8 teaspoon

dice: to cut food into very small cubes (1/4 inch)

dot: to place small bits of butter, etc., on top of pastry or other dishes

dredge: to coat thoroughly, as with flour

filet (or fillet): 1. a piece of poultry, meat, or fish from which the bones have been removed 2. to cut the bones from a piece of meat or fish

fines herbes: a French term for a mixture of herbs, including parsley, chervil, chives, and tarragon, used as a seasoning

flute: to make decorative indentations, as on the edge of a piecrust

fold: to blend delicate ingredients such as whipped cream or beaten egg whites gently into a heavier mixture

gratin: a dish topped with bread crumbs or cheese mixed with bits of butter, then heated under the broiler or in the oven until crisp and brown

julienne: to slice into thin strips about the size of matchsticks

knead: to work dough with a press-and-fold motion

lard: 1. rendered pork fat used in baking 2. to insert long, thin strips of fat (usually pork) or bacon into a dry cut of meat to make the cooked meat more tender and flavorful

marbled: Meat that is marbled shows visible fat throughout, which makes it tenderer.

marinade: a seasoned liquid in which foods such as meat, fish, and vegetables are soaked, or marinated, until they absorb flavor and become tender

meringue: a mixture of stiffly beaten egg whites and sugar

mince: to cut or grind into very tiny pieces

parboil: to boil for a short period of time, until partially cooked

poach: to cook in simmering liquid

purée: to push food through a fine sieve or blend in a food processor until smooth and very thick

sauté: to cook food quickly in a skillet over direct heat using a small amount of oil or fat

scald: to heat liquid to just below the boiling point

score: to make shallow cuts in the surface of certain foods, such as meat or fish

simmer: to cook food in liquid over low heat maintained just below the boiling point

steam: to cook food over boiling water in a covered pan with holes in the bottom to let steam through

truss: to secure poultry with string or skewers so that it holds its shape while cooking

whip: to introduce air into a mixture by beating rapidly with a hand beater, whisk, or electric beater

zest: the aromatic outermost skin layer of citrus fruit. Only the colored portion of the skin is used, as the white pith has a bitter flavor.

EMERGENCY SUBSTITUTIONS

baking powder, double-acting
1 teaspoon (5 ml) = 1 teaspoon (5 ml) baking soda plus
1/2 teaspoon (2.5 ml) cream of tartar.

brown sugar
1 cup (198 g) = 1 cup granulated sugar (198 g),
2 tablespoons (30 ml) molasses or treacle

buttermilk
1 cup (237 ml) = 1 tablespoon (15 ml) lemon juice or vinegar plus enough milk
to make 1 cup (237 ml) and let stand five minutes, or use 1 cup (237 ml) yogurt

cake flour or extra-fine plain flour
1 cup (100 g) = 1 cup (125 g) all-purpose or plain flour minus 2 tablespoons (16 g).

chocolate, semisweet
1 ounce (30 g) = 1 ounce (30 g) unsweetened chocolate plus
1 tablespoon (12.5 g) sugar

heavy cream (40% fat content)
1 cup (237 ml) = 2/3 cup (158 ml) milk and 1/3 cup (75.6 g) butter

herbs, fresh
1 tablespoon (14 g) fresh herbs = 1 teaspoon (5 ml) dry herbs

egg
1 large egg = ¼ cup (59 ml) commercial liquid egg substitute; or
1 egg white and 2 teaspoons (10 ml) oil; or (in baking) 1/2 teaspoon (2.5 ml)
double-acting baking powder, 1 tablespoon (15 ml) vinegar, and 1 tablespoon
(15 ml) liquid (use whatever liquid the recipe calls for)

egg yolk
1 egg yolk = 2 tablespoons (30 ml) commercial egg substitute

flour, all-purpose or plain
1 cup (125 g) = 1 cup (125 g) plus 2 tablespoons (12.5 g) cake flour
or extra-fine flour

flour, self-rising

1 cup (125 g) = 1 cup (125 g) all-purpose or plain flour plus
1-1/2 teaspoons (7 ml) double-acting baking powder and
1/8 teaspoon (.5 ml) salt

honey

1 cup (340 g) = 1-1/4 cups (247.5 g) granulated sugar plus 1/4 cup (59.25 ml)
liquid (use whatever liquid the recipe calls for)

milk

1 cup (237 ml) = 1/2 cup (118.5 ml) evaporated milk plus
1/2 (118.5 ml) cup water; or use dry, powdered milk and mix
according to directions

sour cream

1 cup (237 ml) = 1 cup (237 ml) plain yogurt

sugar, granulated

1 cup (198 g) = 1 cup (198 g) packed light brown sugar, or
1-3/4 cups (141.25 g) confectioner's (or icing) sugar

APPETIZERS

*Happiness
is a kitchen full
of family.*

INDEX

Recipe	Page

RECIPE ....

Servings .... Prep Time..............................

Source ....

INGREDIENTS

....

....

....

....

....

....

....

....

....

....

....

....

....

....

....

....

INSTRUCTIONS

....
....
....
....
....
....
....
....
....
....
....
....
....
....
....
....

This family recipe is special because...

....
....
....

RECIPE ....

Servings .... Prep Time ....

Source ....

INGREDIENTS

....

....

....

....

....

....

....

....

....

....

....

....

....

....

....

....

INSTRUCTIONS

....

....

....

....

....

....

....

....

....

....

....

....

....

....

....

This family recipe is special because...

....

....

....

RECIPE...

Servings .... Prep Time..................................

Source ....

INGREDIENTS

....

....

....

....

....

....

....

....

....

....

....

....

....

....

....

....

INSTRUCTIONS

....
....
....
....
....
....
....
....
....
....
....
....
....
....

This family recipe is special because...

....
....
....

RECIPE ....

Servings .... Prep Time ....

Source ....

INGREDIENTS

....

....

....

....

....

....

....

....

....

....

....

....

....

....

....

....

INSTRUCTIONS

....

....

....

....

....

....

....

....

....

....

....

....

....

....

This family recipe is special because...

....

....

....

RECIPE ....

Servings .... Prep Time ....

Source ....

INGREDIENTS

....

....

....

....

....

....

....

....

....

....

....

....

....

....

....

....

INSTRUCTIONS

....
....
....
....
....
....
....
....
....
....
....
....
....
....
....
....

This family recipe is special because...

....
....
....

RECIPE..

Servings .... Prep Time...

Source..

INGREDIENTS

....

....

....

....

....

....

....

....

....

....

....

....

....

....

....

....

INSTRUCTIONS

....
....
....
....
....
....
....
....
....
....
....
....
....
....

This family recipe is special because...

....
....
....

RECIPE...

Servings .... Prep Time.............................

Source ....

INGREDIENTS

....

....

....

....

....

....

....

....

....

....

....

....

....

....

....

....

....

INSTRUCTIONS

....

....

....

....

....

....

....

....

....

....

....

....

....

....

....

This family recipe is special because...

....

....

....

RECIPE ....

Servings .... Prep Time ....

Source ....

INGREDIENTS

....

....

....

....

....

....

....

....

....

....

....

....

....

....

....

....

INSTRUCTIONS

This family recipe is special because...

RECIPE ....

Servings .... Prep Time...............................

Source ....

INGREDIENTS

....
....
....
....
....
....
....
....
....
....
....
....
....
....
....
....

INSTRUCTIONS

....
....
....
....
....
....
....
....
....
....
....
....
....
....
....
....

This family recipe is special because...

....
....
....

SOUPS, SALADS, & SANDWICHES

Cooking with kids is not just about ingredients, recipes, and cooking. It's about harnessing imagination, empowerment, and creativity.

Guy Fieri

INDEX

Recipe	Page

RECIPE...

Servings .... Prep Time.................................

Source ....

INGREDIENTS

....

....

....

....

....

....

....

....

....

....

....

....

....

....

....

....

INSTRUCTIONS

This family recipe is special because...

RECIPE..

Servings .... Prep Time..............................

Source ....

INGREDIENTS

....

....

....

....

....

....

....

....

....

....

....

....

....

....

....

....

INSTRUCTIONS

....

....

....

....

....

....

....

....

....

....

....

....

....

....

This family recipe is special because...

....

....

....

RECIPE..

Servings .... Prep Time...............................

Source..

INGREDIENTS

....

....

....

....

....

....

....

....

....

....

....

....

....

....

....

....

....

INSTRUCTIONS

....
....
....
....
....
....
....
....
....
....
....
....
....
....
....
....

This family recipe is special because...

....
....
....

RECIPE..

Servings .... Prep Time.............................

Source...

INGREDIENTS

....

....

....

....

....

....

....

....

....

....

....

....

....

....

....

....

INSTRUCTIONS

....
....
....
....
....
....
....
....
....
....
....
....
....
....
....

This family recipe is special because...

....
....
....

RECIPE ....

Servings .... Prep Time ....

Source ....

INGREDIENTS

....

....

....

....

....

....

....

....

....

....

....

....

....

....

....

....

....

INSTRUCTIONS

....
....
....
....
....
....
....
....
....
....
....
....
....
....
....

This family recipe is special because...

....
....
....

RECIPE ....

Servings .... Prep Time ....

Source ....

INGREDIENTS

....

....

....

....

....

....

....

....

....

....

....

....

....

....

....

....

INSTRUCTIONS

This family recipe is special because...

RECIPE ....

Servings .... Prep Time ....

Source ....

INGREDIENTS

....

....

....

....

....

....

....

....

....

....

....

....

....

....

....

INSTRUCTIONS

This family recipe is special because...

RECIPE..

Servings .... Prep Time.............................

Source ....

INGREDIENTS

....

....

....

....

....

....

....

....

....

....

....

....

....

....

....

....

INSTRUCTIONS

This family recipe is special because...

RECIPE ....

Servings .... Prep Time...............................

Source ....

INGREDIENTS

....

....

....

....

....

....

....

....

....

....

....

....

....

....

....

....

....

INSTRUCTIONS

....
....
....
....
....
....
....
....
....
....
....
....
....
....
....
....

This family recipe is special because...

....
....
....

SIDE DISHES

The most remarkable
thing about my mother is
that for thirty years
she served the family nothing
but leftovers.
The original meal
has never been found.

Calvin Trillin

INDEX

Recipe   Page

RECIPE..

Servings .... Prep Time.............................

Source ....

INGREDIENTS

....	....
....	....
....	....
....	....
....	....
....	....
....	....
....	....
....	....
....	....
....	....
....	....
....	....
....	....
....	....
....	....

INSTRUCTIONS

....
....
....
....
....
....
....
....
....
....
....
....
....
....
....

This family recipe is special because...

....
....
....

RECIPE..

Servings .... Prep Time................................

Source ....

INGREDIENTS

....

....

....

....

....

....

....

....

....

....

....

....

....

....

....

....

....

INSTRUCTIONS

....

....

....

....

....

....

....

....

....

....

....

....

....

....

....

This family recipe is special because...

....

....

....

RECIPE...

Servings .... Prep Time...

Source...

INGREDIENTS

....　..

....　..

....　..

....　..

....　..

....　..

....　..

....　..

....　..

....　..

....　..

....　..

....　..

....　..

....　..

....　..

....　..

INSTRUCTIONS

....
....
....
....
....
....
....
....
....
....
....
....
....
....
....
....

This family recipe is special because...

....
....
....

RECIPE ....

Servings .... Prep Time ....

Source ....

INGREDIENTS

....

....

....

....

....

....

....

....

....

....

....

....

....

....

....

....

INSTRUCTIONS

....

....

....

....

....

....

....

....

....

....

....

....

....

....

....

This family recipe is special because...

....

....

....

RECIPE ....

Servings .... Prep Time...

Source ....

INGREDIENTS

....

....

....

....

....

....

....

....

....

....

....

....

....

....

....

....

INSTRUCTIONS

....

....

....

....

....

....

....

....

....

....

....

....

....

....

....

....

....

This family recipe is special because...

....

....

....

RECIPE..

Servings .... Prep Time...

Source...

INGREDIENTS

....

....

....

....

....

....

....

....

....

....

....

....

....

....

....

....

INSTRUCTIONS

....
....
....
....
....
....
....
....
....
....
....
....
....
....
....
....
....
....

This family recipe is special because...

....
....
....

RECIPE ....

Servings .... Prep Time...............................

Source ....

INGREDIENTS

....

....

....

....

....

....

....

....

....

....

....

....

....

....

....

....

INSTRUCTIONS

This family recipe is special because...

RECIPE...

Servings .... Prep Time...............................

Source...

INGREDIENTS

....

....

....

....

....

....

....

....

....

....

....

....

....

....

....

....

INSTRUCTIONS

....

....

....

....

....

....

....

....

....

....

....

....

....

....

This family recipe is special because...

....

....

....

RECIPE..

Servings .... Prep Time..

Source...

INGREDIENTS

....
....
....
....
....
....
....
....
....
....
....
....
....
....
....
....

INSTRUCTIONS

....

....

....

....

....

....

....

....

....

....

....

....

....

....

This family recipe is special because...

....

....

....

MAIN COURSES

They say that gardens look
better when they are created
by loving gardeners rather
than by landscapers, because
the garden is more tended to
and cared for.
The same thing goes for cooking.
I only cook for people I love.

Ina Garten

INDEX

Recipe

Page

RECIPE ....

Servings .... Prep Time.............................

Source ....

INGREDIENTS

....

....

....

....

....

....

....

....

....

....

....

....

....

....

....

....

....

....

INSTRUCTIONS

....

....

....

....

....

....

....

....

....

....

....

....

....

....

This family recipe is special because...

....

....

....

RECIPE ....

Servings .... Prep Time ....

Source ....

INGREDIENTS

....

....

....

....

....

....

....

....

....

....

....

....

....

....

....

....

INSTRUCTIONS

....
....
....
....
....
....
....
....
....
....
....
....
....
....
....
....

This family recipe is special because...

....
....
....

RECIPE ....

Servings .... Prep Time.................................

Source ....

INGREDIENTS

....

....

....

....

....

....

....

....

....

....

....

....

....

....

....

....

INSTRUCTIONS

....
....
....
....
....
....
....
....
....
....
....
....
....
....

This family recipe is special because...

....
....
....

RECIPE..

Servings .... Prep Time................................

Source ....

INGREDIENTS

....
....
....
....
....
....
....
....
....
....
....
....
....
....
....
....
....

INSTRUCTIONS

....

....

....

....

....

....

....

....

....

....

....

....

....

....

....

....

This family recipe is special because...

....

....

....

RECIPE ....

Servings .... Prep Time ....

Source ....

INGREDIENTS

....	....
....	....
....	....
....	....
....	....
....	....
....	....
....	....
....	....
....	....
....	....
....	....
....	....
....	....
....	....
....	....
....	....

INSTRUCTIONS

This family recipe is special because...

RECIPE...

Servings .... Prep Time.......................................

Source...

INGREDIENTS

....
....
....
....
....
....
....
....
....
....
....
....
....
....
....
....
....

INSTRUCTIONS

....
....
....
....
....
....
....
....
....
....
....
....
....
....

This family recipe is special because...

....
....
....

RECITE..

Servings .... Prep Time..

Source..

INGREDIENTS

....

....

....

....

....

....

....

....

....

....

....

....

....

....

....

....

INSTRUCTIONS

....

....

....

....

....

....

....

....

....

....

....

....

....

....

....

This family recipe is special because...

....

....

....

RECIPE..

Servings .... Prep Time.............................

Source ....

INGREDIENTS

....

....

....

....

....

....

....

....

....

....

....

....

....

....

....

....

....

INSTRUCTIONS

....

....

....

....

....

....

....

....

....

....

....

....

....

....

....

This family recipe is special because...

....

....

....

RECIPE...

Servings .... Prep Time...............................

Source ....

INGREDIENTS

....
....
....
....
....
....
....
....
....
....
....
....
....
....
....
....

INSTRUCTIONS

....

....

....

....

....

....

....

....

....

....

....

....

....

....

This family recipe is special because...

....

....

....

DESSERTS

Families are like fudge—
mostly sweet with
a few nuts.

Author unknown

INDEX

Recipe   Page

RECIPE...

Servings .... Prep Time...........................

Source ....

INGREDIENTS

....

....

....

....

....

....

....

....

....

....

....

....

....

....

....

....

INSTRUCTIONS

....
....
....
....
....
....
....
....
....
....
....
....
....
....
....
....
....

This family recipe is special because...

....
....
....

RECIPE ....

Servings .... Prep Time ....

Source ....

INGREDIENTS

....
....
....
....
....
....
....
....
....
....
....
....
....
....
....
....
....

INSTRUCTIONS

This family recipe is special because...

RECIPE ....

Servings .... Prep Time...............................

Source ....

INGREDIENTS

....

....

....

....

....

....

....

....

....

....

....

....

....

....

....

....

INSTRUCTIONS

....
....
....
....
....
....
....
....
....
....
....
....
....
....

This family recipe is special because...

....
....
....

RECIPE..

Servings .... Prep Time..

Source...

INGREDIENTS

....

....

....

....

....

....

....

....

....

....

....

....

....

....

....

....

INSTRUCTIONS

This family recipe is special because...

RECIPE..

Servings .... Prep Time.............................

Source ....

INGREDIENTS

....

....

....

....

....

....

....

....

....

....

....

....

....

....

....

....

INSTRUCTIONS

....
....
....
....
....
....
....
....
....
....
....
....
....
....
....
....

This family recipe is special because...

....
....
....

RECIPE ....

Servings .... Prep Time ....

Source ....

INGREDIENTS

....

....

....

....

....

....

....

....

....

....

....

....

....

....

....

....

INSTRUCTIONS

....

....

....

....

....

....

....

....

....

....

....

....

....

....

....

....

This family recipe is special because...

....

....

....

RECIPE ....

Servings .... Prep Time.............................

Source ....

INGREDIENTS

....	....
....	....
....	....
....	....
....	....
....	....
....	....
....	....
....	....
....	....
....	....
....	....
....	....
....	....
....	....
....	....
....	....

INSTRUCTIONS

....

....

....

....

....

....

....

....

....

....

....

....

....

....

This family recipe is special because...

....

....

....

RECIPE ....

Servings .... Prep Time ....

Source ....

INGREDIENTS

....

....

....

....

....

....

....

....

....

....

....

....

....

....

....

....

INSTRUCTIONS

....
....
....
....
....
....
....
....
....
....
....
....
....
....
....

This family recipe is special because...

....
....
....

RECIPE ....

Servings .... Prep Time................................

Source ....

INGREDIENTS

....

....

....

....

....

....

....

....

....

....

....

....

....

....

....

....

INSTRUCTIONS

....
....
....
....
....
....
....
....
....
....
....
....
....
....
....

This family recipe is special because...

....
....
....

BEVERAGES

I come from a family
where gravy is considered
a beverage.

Erma Bombeck

INDEX

Recipe

Page

....

....

....

....

....

....

....

....

RECIPE ....

Servings .... Prep Time ....

Source ....

INGREDIENTS

....

....

....

....

....

....

....

....

....

....

....

....

....

....

....

....

....

INSTRUCTIONS

....

....

....

....

....

....

....

....

....

....

....

....

....

....

....

This family recipe is special because...

....

....

....

RECIPE..

Servings .... Prep Time................................

Source...

INGREDIENTS

....	....
....	....
....	....
....	....
....	....
....	....
....	....
....	....
....	....
....	....
....	....
....	....
....	....
....	....
....	....
....	....

INSTRUCTIONS

....
....
....
....
....
....
....
....
....
....
....
....
....
....
....
....

This family recipe is special because...

....
....
....

RECIPE..

Servings .... Prep Time...

Source ....

INGREDIENTS

....

....

....

....

....

....

....

....

....

....

....

....

....

....

....

....

....

INSTRUCTIONS

....

....

....

....

....

....

....

....

....

....

....

....

....

....

....

This family recipe is special because...

....

....

....

RECITE ....

Servings .... Prep Time..............................

Source ....

INGREDIENTS

....

....

....

....

....

....

....

....

....

....

....

....

....

....

....

....

INSTRUCTIONS

....

....

....

....

....

....

....

....

....

....

....

....

....

....

....

This family recipe is special because...

....

....

....

RECIPE ....

Servings .... Prep Time ....

Source ....

INGREDIENTS

....

....

....

....

....

....

....

....

....

....

....

....

....

....

....

....

....

INSTRUCTIONS

This family recipe is special because...

RECIPE ....

Servings .... Prep Time ....

Source ....

INGREDIENTS

....

....

....

....

....

....

....

....

....

....

....

....

....

....

....

....

INSTRUCTIONS

....

....

....

....

....

....

....

....

....

....

....

....

....

....

....

....

This family recipe is special because...

....

....

....

RECIPE ....

Servings .... Prep Time................................

Source ....

INGREDIENTS

....
....
....
....
....
....
....
....
....
....
....
....
....
....
....
....
....

INSTRUCTIONS

This family recipe is special because...

RECIPE...

Servings .... Prep Time...

Source...

INGREDIENTS

....

....

....

....

....

....

....

....

....

....

....

....

....

....

....

....

....

INSTRUCTIONS

This family recipe is special because...

RECIPE..

Servings .... Prep Time..

Source ....

INGREDIENTS

....

....

....

....

....

....

....

....

....

....

....

....

....

....

....

....

....

INSTRUCTIONS

....
....
....
....
....
....
....
....
....
....
....
....
....
....
....
....
....
....

This family recipe is special because...

....
....
....

MORE RECIPES

*Family life is a bit like
a runny peach pie—
not perfect but
who's complaining?*

Robert Brault

INDEX

Recipe	Page

RECIPE..

Servings .... Prep Time..............................

Source...

INGREDIENTS

....

....

....

....

....

....

....

....

....

....

....

....

....

....

....

INSTRUCTIONS

This family recipe is special because...

RECIPE ....

Servings .... Prep Time ....

Source ....

INGREDIENTS

....

....

....

....

....

....

....

....

....

....

....

....

....

....

....

....

INSTRUCTIONS

This family recipe is special because...

RECIPE..

Servings .... Prep Time..

Source...

INGREDIENTS

....

....

....

....

....

....

....

....

....

....

....

....

....

....

....

....

INSTRUCTIONS

....

....

....

....

....

....

....

....

....

....

....

....

....

....

....

....

This family recipe is special because...

....

....

....

RECIPE ....

Servings .... Prep Time ....

Source ....

INGREDIENTS

....

....

....

....

....

....

....

....

....

....

....

....

....

....

....

....

INSTRUCTIONS

This family recipe is special because...

RECIPE ....

Servings .... Prep Time ....

Source ....

INGREDIENTS

....

....

....

....

....

....

....

....

....

....

....

....

....

....

....

....

INSTRUCTIONS

This family recipe is special because...

NOTES